T0198423

God's First Christmas Gift

Betty Brown

Archway Publishing books may be ordered through booksellers or by contacting:

Archway Publishing
1663 Liberty Drive
Bloomington, IN 47403
www.archwaypublishing.com
844-669-3957

Because of the dynamic nature of the Internet, any web addresses or links contained in this book may have changed since publication and may no longer be valid. The views expressed in this work are solely those of the author and do not necessarily reflect the views of the publisher, and the publisher hereby disclaims any responsibility for them.

Any people depicted in stock imagery provided by Getty Images are models, and such images are being used for illustrative purposes only.
Certain stock imagery © Getty Images.

Scripture taken from the New King James Version®. Copyright © 1982 by Thomas Nelson. Used by permission. All rights reserved.

ISBN: 978-1-6657-0569-1 (sc)
ISBN: 978-1-6657-0570-7 (hc)
ISBN: 978-1-6657-0571-4 (e)

Print information available on the last page.

Archway Publishing rev. date: 05/07/2021

God's First
Christmas Gift

"And she will bring forth a Son, and you shall call His name Jesus, for He will save His people from their sins."

Matthew 1:21

A long time ago in a land far away,

Lived a good man named Joseph who was happy all day.

One night as Joseph was alone,

An angel was sent from God's heavenly throne

Who said: "Fear not to take Mary as your wife,

And you will be happy the rest of your life.

She will have a baby boy

Who will bring you happiness and great joy!

He won't be an ordinary child as you will see;

His name shall be Jesus, and He'll set all men free."

Then Joseph said, "I'll gladly obey,"

And he took Mary to be his bride right away.

Joseph took Mary to Bethlehem,

Where she would have her baby then.

He knocked on many doors that day

To see if there was a place to stay.

Mary would have her baby soon,

And Joseph wanted a lovely room.

But Bethlehem was crowded as could be.

There wasn't a single room left free.

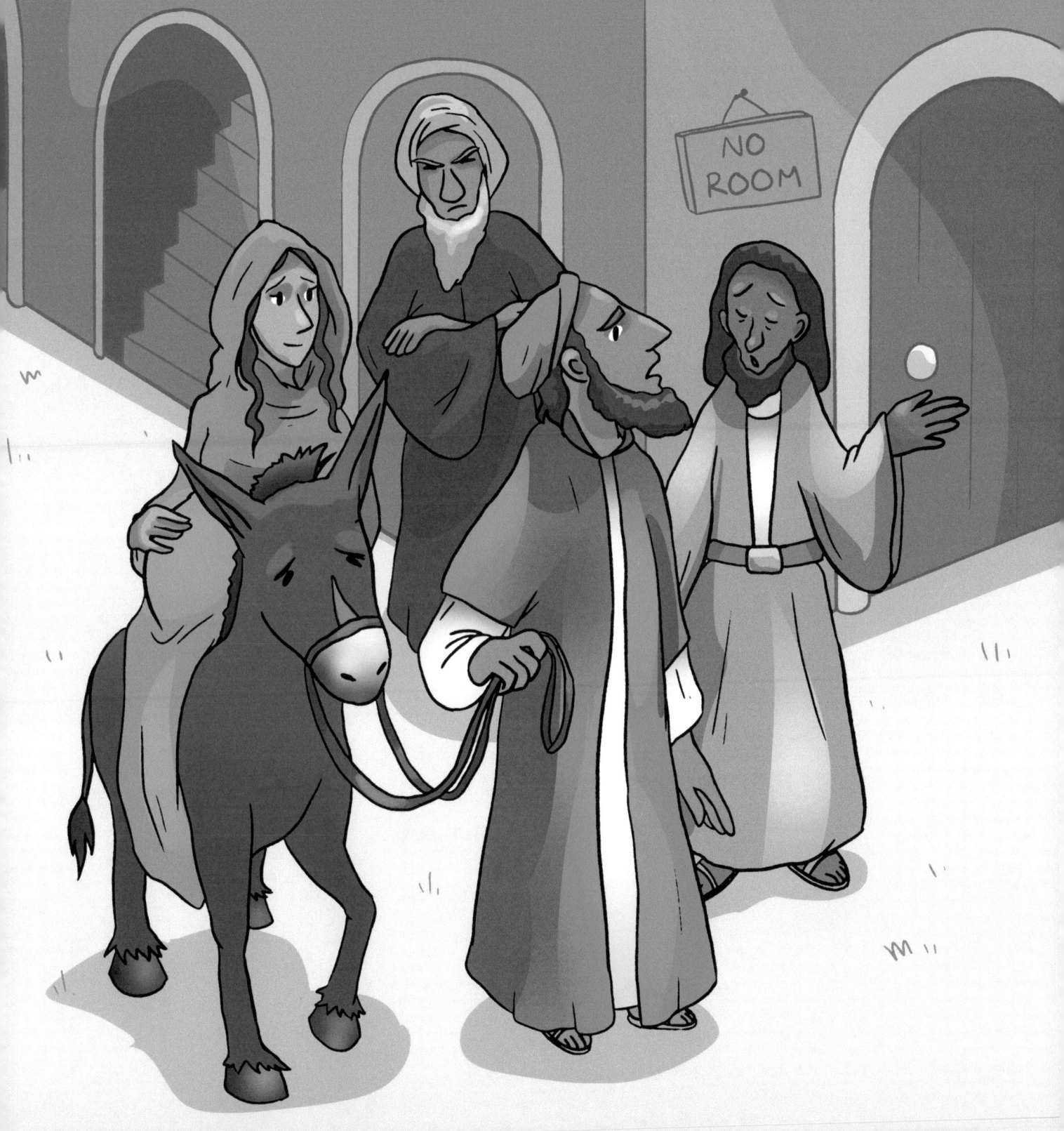

"Go away!" one said. "Don't bother me.

There's no room in this inn. Can't you see?"

And another said "No room in my inn, but how about my shed?

Why not go there to make your bed?"

So Joseph took Mary to the shed

And made a manger for the baby's bed.

She had God's baby on that night,

And over them stood a star so bright.

Some very wise men came to Herod to say

"We saw a strange sight in the sky today!

A star so large and so very bright,

We knew that Jesus was born somewhere that night."

So they followed the star all the way.

They followed at night and they followed by day.

On and on they travelled so far,

And going before them was that star.

Until it came to the one they loved,

God's only Son sent from heaven above.

The star stood still where the baby lay,

And the wise men fell on their faces to pray.

They cried with happiness and great joy

When they saw God's Son a baby boy!

At that same time shepherds watched their sheep at night

When lo, the angel of the Lord shone bright!

The shepherds were sore afraid. Not a single noise they made.

But the angel said, "Do not be afraid for behold I bring good news today".

I bring good tidings of great joy.

Unto you is born a baby boy.

He is God's only Son. Jesus has come to save everyone."

The angels went away with great singing.

And the shepherd's hearts were rejoicing and ringing.

Run, run as fast as you can. You can't catch us.

We're going to Bethlehem!

They too saw the star shining so bright

And arrived quickly at the manger site.

Wise men with gifts, angels, cattle and sheep,

Donkeys and doves lay at Jesus' feet.

The shepherds came and then they knew

What God's angel had told them was certainly true.

They found Joseph and Mary and the small little child,

Jesus, God's Son, so gentle and mild.

The baby lying there in the manger

Would soon grow up to save us from danger.

What a wonder. It really is true.

Glory and praises to God for this gift so new!

They could not wait to go tell everyone.

Jesus is born! Jesus is born! God's own Son.

And may we like the shepherds that wonderful night

Tell all of our friends of His goodness and might.

About the Author

Betty Brown began working with preschool children, in 1971, while living in California. After moving to New Jersey, she taught Kindergarten in a private Christian school for 20 years and then opened her "Little Stars" home school. Betty is especially gifted in storytelling either Biblical or classics. She has also had the privilege of having been Director of Vacation Bible School for 24 years with 200 plus children in attendance. She has conducted Children's Church, the Academy Chorus, as well as Talent Night for teens. Betty has been involved in numerous speaking engagements for women's retreats as well as Women's Aglow. She is presently involved in women's Bible studies in her church and also in her home. Her hobbies include reading, writing and playing the cello. She started cello lessons at age six and has played in orchestras in New Jersey and California. Presently, she plays on the worship team at her church. She and her husband, Bill, are retired and enjoying their adult children and eight grandchildren.

Printed in the United States
by Baker & Taylor Publisher Services